STEAM COLOUR PORTFOLIO

Eastern & North Eastern Region

VOLUME ONE

Keith R.Pirt

BOOK LAW PUBLICATIONS

First published in the United Kingdom by Book Law Publications 2005
382 Carlton Hill, Nottingham, NG4 1JA
Printed and bound by The Amadeus Press, Cleckheaton, West Yorkshire.

Introduction

Keith Pirt travelled the length and breadth of the country in his quest to capture the right subjects on perfectly placed slides in perfect weather. Of course he had his favourite 'spots' be they close to home or far flung in Scotland or the west of England. He did not visit everywhere, at least in the days when he concentrated on his colour work, so do not expect to see too many views in the Birmingham, Bradford or Manchester areas in colour (we will explore his earlier far reaching black and white work in a new series which is to be published later). Instead, savour the places where he liked to go, be they lineside or on some engine shed or locomotive works yard.

KRP was essentially a locomotive and train photographer who appreciated the diversity of rolling stock but did not record any on film. He did not photograph, in colour anyway, stations, engine sheds, signal boxes or the like unless of course a train was included. However, what he did capture for us is worth study. He spent many hours at the lineside waiting for the train which, in his mind, had the best exhaust and, having already 'set up his stall', he would commit that particular shot to film. He was simply a perfectionist.

This particular volume features a diverse selection of locomotive classes at work and at rest in a number far reaching geographical locations which range from western Scotland to East Anglia and everywhere in between. Pacifics tend to dominate but not overwhelm this album and other lesser locomotive types are included to bring you a nice cocktail worthy of the excellent photography. So, sit back, relax and enjoy some of the best colour photography reflecting the last decade of steam on British Railways.

LOCOMOTIVES FEATURED IN THIS VOLUME:

60002, 60005, 60006, 60008, 60009, 60010, 60013, 60017, 60021, 60023, 60028, 60029, 60031, 60044, 60047, 60052, 60054, 60062, 60063, 60067, 60070, 60080, 60102, 4472, 60107, 60108, 60110, 60111, 60112, 60115, 60119, 60128, 60131, 60142, 60146, 60156, 60500, 60501, 60516, 60524, 60530, 60533, 60816, 60820, 60837, 60846, 60867, 60893, 60895, 60974, 61087, 61152, 61190, 61208, 61211, 61334, 61384, 61402, 61425, 61626, 2005, 62015, 62061, 62387, 62589, 62663, 62669, 62785, 63655, 63795, 63824, 63914, 63933, 63936, 63939, 63945, 63980, 64332, 64547, 64577, 64672, 64689, 65313, 65882, 67340, 67417, 68736, 68784, 69477, 69523, 69854.

Long before the National Railway Museum was created from its bones, Leeman Road engine shed at York was home to many of the ECML V2's, including No.60837 which is seen outside the shed in June 1963 taking water. During the late summer and early autumn of 1959 this engine worked from Leeds Copley Hill shed but for the rest of its twenty-seven year life No.60837 was a York based V2. Condemned as late as 16th November 1965, No.60837 was sold for scrap to Cox & Danks at Wadsley Bridge a month later. *(BLP - E932)*

Making its way home in October 1961, New England V2 No.60893 storms past Ordsall with an Up fitted freight. Built in January 1940, this V2, with a couple of minor exceptions, had spent most of its life working from New England shed. The exceptions were a fourteen month spell at Grantham shed from October 1957 to December 1958 and, perhaps more unusually, a six week loan to the Southern Region from 14th May to the end of June 1953. The reason for the latter transfer was to help that Region out when it had a locomotive shortage due to the temporary withdrawal of all their 'Merchant Navy' Pacifics. Less than a year after the date of this photograph, No.60893 was condemned and shortly before Christmas 1962 it went into Doncaster works for breaking up. *(BLP - E933)*

Not too many A3's in this album, especially with the German type smoke deflectors, so its nice to have this one of No.60044 MELTON as its nears Brookmans Park with an afternoon Leeds to King's Cross express in September 1961. The A3 had just finished a 'General' overhaul (its last) on 30th August at which shopping it acquired the smoke deflectors. Since being rebuilt from Class A10 in September 1947, No.60044 had certainly 'done the rounds' regarding shed allocations with all of the major sheds on the old Great Northern main line attended and even a couple of the old Great Central establishments 'under its belt' - Leicester and Neasden. Except for a week in 1924 when it was briefly used by Gorton shed in Manchester, the Pacific, then numbered LNER 2543, had spent the twenty-three years up to its rebuilding, shedded at depots situated within the boundary of the old GNR. Built at Doncaster, maintained at Doncaster, No.60044 was cut up at Doncaster during the winter of 1963. *(BLP - E304)*

(opposite) Cambridge based E4 No.62785 rounds the curve out of Fordham station with an afternoon Mildenhall branch train in May 1958. No.62785 was of course the lucky one and is preserved, however, when this scene was captured we are sure that preservation was hardly mentioned, if at all, for this locomotive. A resume of its history shows that it was put into traffic in January 1895 from Stratford works after the design of James Holden. No less than one hundred of these useful 2-4-0 tender engines became LNER property with the oldest of them being thirty-two years old in 1923. That so many of the class should reach British Railways ownership is surely a tribute to their designer. During the LNER and BR periods No.62785 had four stints at Cambridge shed where it spent most of its later life. Other sheds where it resided for shorter periods were Bury St Edmunds, Hitchin and Norwich. The engine's Great Eastern number was 490, followed by the LNER addition of 7000 in the early 1920's. In November 1942 it was changed from 7490 to 7802 and in December 1946 it became 2785 under the Thompson 1943 renumbering scheme. Condemned 7th December 1959, the rest of its life is public knowledge. What of the route used by the E4? Well, Fordham station closed in 1965 whilst the Mildenhall branch had closed some three years earlier along with the direct branch line from Barnwell Junction to Fordham. *(BLP - E301)*

With what might have been regarded then as a Copley Hill based Peppercorn A1 turn, King's Cross based Gresley A3 No.60110 ROBERT THE DEVIL (what wonderful names these engines carried and, what might have been the alternative if Doncaster did not have a racecourse?) heads the Down *YORKSHIRE PULLMAN*, with no headboard, through Brookmans Park in May 1961. The engine had just received a 'Casual Light' repair at Doncaster works, its second to last such repair prior to withdrawal. Rebuilt from an A1 in 1942, this engine was married to the same tender (No.5230) throughout its life, the only Gresley A1 to do so. Condemned in may 1963, the A3 was cut up at Doncaster works the following month. *(BLP - E336)*

(opposite) When the LNER purchased large numbers of the Ministry of Munitions version of the Robinson O4 during the 1920's, they knew that what they had bought would last them a long time. However, the design outlasted the life of the Company and, in its various rebuilt state, the O4 went on working until the end of steam on the former LNER section of British Railways. O4 Part 7 No.63824, seen here beside the south wall of Retford GC engine shed in March 1961, was one of the forty-eight acquired from the Government in February 1925 for £1,500 each. That batch were not the cheapest though and exactly two years later the LNER got hold of another one hundred O4's for just £340 each! No.63824 began its LNER career at the end of March 1926 after a 'General' overhaul at Gorton works. It was then numbered 6516 and had been built in November 1918 by the North British Locomotive Co. from the start the engine worked over the former Great Central lines, being allocated to places such as Sheffield, Scunthorpe, Barnsley and Retford. Originally the engine was classified O4 Part 1 but was rebuilt in May 1943 to Part 7 which entailed fitting a new boiler (Diagram 15D) with a round top firebox, similar to the Gresley O2 engines. No.63824 had undergone a 'General' at Gorton during the previous October and which probably accounts for its reasonable appearance here. Condemned in June 1963, the engine was cut up at Doncaster works a month later. *(BLP - E314)*

Sitting by the East Coast Main Line at High Dyke on an August afternoon was probably one of the nicest methods of relaxation known to most enthusiasts and Keith Pirt spent many of his summer afternoons 'lineside' so that scenes such as this were captured for posterity and future enjoyment. In 1962 this Doncaster based Peppercorn A1, No.60119 PATRICK STIRLING, was working north with an express during the last summer when steam motive power would be passing through here in any number. Already the diesels were making their mark and had virtually taken over all the named expresses from the Pacific's. No.60119 had gone through its last 'General' repair just five months previously and would not visit works again until withdrawal at the end of May 1964. It was sold privately for scrap in August of that year. *(BLP - E318)*

Now, having mentioned in the previous caption that the main line diesels had taken over the haulage of virtually every ECML named train by August 1962, here is one that they had not - yet! Yes it is August 1962, the place is Grantham, and the train is the *ANGLO-SCOTTISH CAR CARRIER*, albeit sans headboard. The locomotive, well that was A4 No.60017 SILVER FOX, one of the original 1935-built members of the class. Now it is August remember and 60017 had completed its last 'General' overhaul during the previous April - 12th April to be exact. It had been in traffic for at least four months but to look at the state of the paintwork you would think the locomotive was working back to its home shed at King's Cross straight after release from works. Therein lies the clue as to why the engine is so clean - allocated to 34A. This A4 retained its original corridor tender (No.5592) throughout it life except for two weeks in summer 1939 when it 'borrowed' another corridor type (No.5642) which was ex MALLARD but afterwards was attached to PEREGRINE. When King's Cross shed closed in June 1963 No.60017 was reallocated to New England shed where, four months later, it was condemned. Doncaster was its birthplace and appropriately, in December 1963, it was taken to pieces there and laid to rest. *(BLP - E319)*

In its last year of operation Thompson A2/2 No.60501 COCK O' THE NORTH was still undertaking secondary express duties from York shed and the staff at that depot were managing to keep the locomotive looking reasonably clean as here in May 1959. Keith Pirt caught the engine on camera whilst it was backing off the shed yard and making its way to the station in order to work a Down express forward to Newcastle. Condemned 8th February 1960, the engine was cut up at Doncaster works the same month - another one best forgotten perhaps. However, the nameplates from this engine do live on and when offered for sale can command large amounts of money, and a lot more respect than the engine ever did, at least in its Pacific guise. *(BLP - E381)*

(opposite) This classic scene was captured at York in October 1964 as the sun shone through the smoky atmosphere inside York shed. Roundhouse sheds, with their lofty roofs and given the right conditions such as this, were ideal for photography. Around the turntable are Peppercorn A1 No.60146 PEREGRINE (the name taken off A4 No.60034 in March 1948), Thompson B1 No.61276, and J27 No.65894. All three were still active and were resident. Long after the other two had been condemned in 1965, the J27 moved to Sunderland for its last stint of working before withdrawal and eventual preservation. *(BLP - E906)*

In excellent afternoon sunshine, during March 1961, A3 No.60054 PRINCE OF WALES races through Tuxford with a northbound express. In the background can be seen the LD&ECR overbridge which by now was devoid of its Dukeries Junction station buildings. No.60054 would have coupled onto this train at Grantham after replacing a King's Cross engine. *(BLP - E914)*

Considering it had been over two years since its last general overhaul and a repaint, N1 No.69477 looks remarkably smart at Copley Hill shed in August 1958. The 0-6-2T had been resident at the Leeds depot since June of the previous year after spending most of its forty-seven year life working from sheds at the southern end of the former Great Northern main line. It had spent two years at Copley Hill before, from September 1952 to August 1954, so was no stranger to the workings radiating from Leeds (Central) station. Indeed the N1 class as a whole were a common sight in the West Riding of Yorkshire with a large proportion of them, thirty by early BR days, stationed at Ardsley, Bradford and Leeds. No.69477 was one of those originally built with condensing apparatus and most of those which had transferred away from the London area kept the gear in situ, although blanked off, whilst just a few had it removed completely. This N1 kept it to the end which came just seven months after this view was captured. It went into Doncaster works for a minor repair at the end of March 1959 but was condemned on the 2nd April and then cut up later that month. *(BLP - E346)*

It seems incredible that this picture of preserved Gresley A3 No.4472 FLYING SCOTSMAN was taken in September 1964 - forty-odd years ago. Anyway the location is Basingstoke on the former Berks. & Hants line from Reading, near to where the GWR joined the Southern main line. The occasion was the Farnborough Air Show with the Pacific in charge of a special train run for the day under the name of the *FARNBOROUGH FLYER PULLMAN*. After detraining its passengers, No.4472 spent the day on Basingstoke shed which although officially closed was still maintained as a servicing point for visiting locomotives. *(BLP - E347)*

A recent acquisition of Aberdeen Ferryhill shed, A4 No.60006 SIR RALPH WEDGWOOD steams towards Gleneagles station on the former Caledonian main line with the Up *WEST COAST POSTAL* in September 1964. One of the early 1938 built A4's, the engine was originally named HERRING GULL and numbered 4466. Its name was changed to the LNER Director in January 1944 whilst its number changed in January 1946 to 605, then in May that year it became No.6. It got its BR number in December 1948 during a general overhaul at Doncaster works whilst it was allocated to King's Cross shed. A regular performer on the East Coast Main Line, 60006 had a corridor tender for much of the early 1950's and was a regular on the non-stop Edinburgh-London express *THE CAPITALS LIMITED*. In June 1963 with its prestigious work on the ECML taken away by the advent of diesel motive power, the A4 was lucky not to have been withdrawn and was sent to New England shed where it could be used as a main line stand-by engine. During the following October it went north for the last time, firstly to Edinburgh St Margarets shed where it was used on all sorts of jobs including goods turns, then, in May 1964, it went back into main line passenger service after being allocated to Ferryhill shed at Aberdeen to work the 3-hour expresses from Aberdeen to Glasgow. Some fourteen A4's spent time at Ferryhill shed during the period from May 1962 to September 1966. Of that final band, no less than four of them were to be preserved - alas No.60006 was not one of them, it was condemned on 3rd September 1965 and was cut up at the Wishaw yard of the Motherwell Machinery & Scrap company. Finally, exLNER designed locomotives were no strangers on the former Caledonian main line or on this particular train. During 1951-53 Peppercorn A1's Nos.60152 HOLYROOD, 60160 AULD REEKIE, 60161 NORTH BRITISH were allocated to Polmadie shed in Glasgow and all of them were regular performers on the Up *WEST COAST POSTAL*. (BLP - E349)

Under a nice clear sky, Peppercorn A1 No.60156 GREAT CENTRAL passes Ordsall, Retford, with the morning Leeds (Central) to King's Cross stopping train in October 1958. From new in October 1949, this engine ran for nearly three years before it was eventually named, the last of the class to be done. No.60156 was first allocated to King's Cross (Top shed) but two years later it moved to Grantham for a five year spell prior to returning to London. In April 1959 Doncaster shed acquired its services until its final move which took it to York in January 1964. Just sixteen years old, the Pacific was condemned in May 1965 and was sold for scrap a month later. (BLP - E341)

(opposite) Fresh from Darlington works where it had been specially painted in North Eastern green with appropriate lining, J72 No.68736 awaits its next shunting job as York station pilot in June 1960. This 0-6-0T could just claim to be a NER engine as it was built in June 1922, six months prior to Grouping. Built by outside contractor Armstrong Whitworth, this engine was amongst the twenty-five not constructed at a railway workshop. At Grouping there were seventy-five J72's in existence but during 1925 another ten engines were constructed and those at Doncaster of all places. Even stranger, resumption of building the J72 started again in 1949 at Darlington when they turned out fifteen engines all with BR numbers. These were followed in 1950 by five more then, in 1951, another eight appeared from the same works. Not bad for a class which first came into traffic in 1898. No.68736 left York for Gateshead shed in July of the following year whence it took up station pilot duties at Newcastle (Central) until withdrawn in October 1963. It was cut up at Darlington the following month. (BLP - E376)

Except for an eight month spell at Neville Hill shed during 1948, the last of the Thompson A2/3's, No.60524 HERRINGBONE had spent all its time from new in September 1947 until December 1962 working from York depot. In March 1959, looking rather splendid, it has charge of an Up afternoon express and is leaving Retford behind on its way south. After it long sojourn at York the Pacific was allocated to Scotland in a move which probably prolonged its life by a couple of years. Arriving first at St Margarets shed on 2nd December 1962, No.60524 moved further north to Ferryhill shed at Aberdeen on New Years Eve then, in September 1963, in one of the strangest moves of the BR period, HERRINGBONE was sent to 66A Polmadie shed for work on the West Coast Main Line. Along with it went two other A2/3's Nos.60512 STEADY AIM and 60522 STRAIGHT DEAL, along with three Peppercorn A2's Nos.60527 SUN CHARIOT, 60530 SAYAJIRAO and 60535 HORNETS BEAUTY - a real bunch of cuckoos. They all worked from the ex Caledonian depot until early 1965 when they were withdrawn on various dates after lying in store for many weeks. No.60524 was condemned 15th February and sold for scrap in May to one of the large scrapyards based in Motherwell. *(BLP E384)*

(opposite) A3 No.60067 LADAS outside Crimpsall shop, Doncaster works, June 1956. Prior to rebuilding from A1 to A3 in 1939, this Pacific had spent all of its life working from Scottish sheds; Haymarket from new in August 1924; Dundee Tay Bridge from August 1930 and finally Eastfield from February 1937. Before transferring to Dundee, No.2566 as the LNER first numbered the engine, was given a 'General' overhaul at Cowlairs works whereupon it was fitted with tablet exchanging apparatus enabling it to work over the single line section of the coast line between Dundee and Aberdeen. Upon rebuilding, which was carried out at Doncaster, the A3 returned to Eastfield but after the outbreak of war it moved firstly to St Margarets shed and then, nine months later, to Haymarket depot where it stayed for another ten years. Leaving Scotland in July 1950, No.60067 then took turns residing at either King's Cross, Grantham, Doncaster or New England sheds. It was condemned at King's Cross shed on 29th December 1962 and entered Doncaster works for scrapping four days later. In this view the engine was in works for a 'Non-classified' repair 9th to 18th June. Alongside, Peppercorn K1 No.62070 is undergoing a similar 'repair' after a 'General' the previous month. *(BLP - E942)*

Passing the somewhat manicured gardens beside Leeman Road carriage sidings, York V2 No.60974, looking rather splendid itself, accelerates northward from York with a heavy Down express in May 1959. Turned out from Darlington works in August 1943, as LNER No.3686, this engine worked for the whole of its short twenty year life from York shed. Condemned in December 1963, it was sent to Darlington for breaking up on 9th January 1964.

(opposite) Here, at Montrose sub shed on a sunny afternoon in June 1966, J37 No.64577 is prepared for duty. Outstationed from Dundee Tay Bridge shed, the 0-6-0 is just weeks away from condemnation on 17th August. Built by North British Locomotive Co. in September 1918, the engine started its working life at Parkhead shed then, in May 1937 it moved to Edinburgh and St Margarets shed. Its next depot was Thornton Junction but that transfer did not take place until December 1962. Just over a week later, having spent New Year in Fife, the J37 steamed north to Dundee where it managed to find work for another three and a half years. Like many of its kin, No.64577 was purchased for its scrap value by the Motherwell Machinery & Scrap Co. and was cut up at their Wishaw yard. Montrose engine shed was erected by the North British Railway in 1881 and the facilities consisted a two-road through type shed with an adjacent coal stage and a turntable large enough to hold an 0-6-0 tender engine. Official closure of the depot had taken place in the May prior to No.64577 using the yard but as was happening during this period of BR's fortunes, the shed remained useable. The actual date of closure is unknown but August or September would be a good guess. *(BLP - E947)*

An early morning departure from York in May 1959 for Darnall based Thompson B1 No.61334 with a York to Bournemouth train. Made up almost exclusively of green painted Southern Region stock, the Eastern Region version would have been leaving Bournemouth at about the same time and making its way home behind a Bullied Pacific. The B1 would take the train probably as far as Nottingham (Victoria) or perhaps Leicester (Central) where, at either station, a former Great Western 4-6-0 would continue southwards with the train as far as Oxford or Reading where a SR 'West Country' or 'Battle of Britain' would take over for the remaining mileage to the south coast resort. *(BLP - E394)*

D16 Part 3 No.62589 was the March station pilot in April 1959. That particular March shed duty carried a label which meant either a locomotive due for 'shopping' or condemnation. No.62589 was ready for the latter and was withdrawn on 18th May prior to being taken to Stratford for breaking up, just a year short of its fiftieth birthday. Starting life at Stratford in July 1910 as Great Eastern No.1818, and part of a class which would become classified on the LNER as a superheated D15, this engine was rebuilt by Stratford to D16 standard just months after Grouping. It was then allocated to Stratford engine shed and would remain so until December 1929 when it went to Southend for seven months. There then followed a three month period when the locomotive was basically shuttled between Southend and Stratford sheds with each depot either claiming it or disowning it, or so it appears. However, on 20th September 1930 Southend shed seems to have won, or lost, and kept hold of No.8818 as the D16 was then identified but in May 1931 Cambridge depot claimed it for the next eleven years. During that time, in late 1933, it was altered to D16 Part 2 standard during a 'General' at Stratford. March shed got the 4-4-0 in December 1942 and it settled down in the Fens for seventeen years working to all points of the compass, north to Doncaster, west to Peterborough and beyond, south to London and east to Norwich and the coast. Between 10th January and 26th March 1947, No.2589 as the engine had now become under the 1946 LNER renumbering scheme, was rebuilt to D16 Part 3 standard, again at Stratford works. It gained its BR number at another 'General' in 1949. Its last major repair was in February 1957 during a period up to May of that year when the last heavy repairs were being given to the class. If No.62589 had been repaired two months later than it was, it would have worn the new BR crest but as can be seen it kept the 'lion and wheel' to the end. *(BLP - E388)*

They just did not look right for some reason or other. Even with the right lighting conditions in perfect weather, something did not seem quite right. The first of Thompson's A2 Part 3 engines No.60500 EDWARD THOMPSON stands at a Down side platform awaiting a northbound departure from Grantham in July 1962. The engine had undergone a 'General' overhaul just three months previously but New England shed, where the engine had moved to from King's Cross in June 1950, made no effort to keep their charges' clean. Before withdrawal in June 1963, this Pacific would make two further visits to Doncaster works for one reason or another. *(BLP - E395)*

Presenting a clean image and just five months before withdrawal, O2 No.63945 takes in the morning sun at Retford Thrumpton engine shed in April 1963. Built in May 1924 as LNER No.3500, this Gresley O2 was allocated to New England shed for its first twenty-one years of life but then moved to Doncaster shed for a year. Langwith Junction engine shed got it fresh from a 'General' in December 1946 by which time its number had changed to 3945. After four years Doncaster shed reclaimed it and kept it until April 1953 when it moved on to Frodingham. Finally, eight months after lodging amongst the steelworks of Scunthorpe, 63945 moved to Retford shed where, for the nearly ten years, it hauled a commodity it was very familiar with - coal. After condemnation the engine was sold to a Nottingham scrapyard. *(BLP - E910)*

Having just moved across the Pennines from Northwich to Sheffield, D11 No.62669 YPRES gets straight down to business handling a Sheffield (Victoria) to Lincoln stopping train in May 1958. By now, these elegant yet powerful 4-4-0s had done all that was asked of them but were relegated to workings' such as this from Darnall shed. At least No.62669 was active; many of its kin were in various states of storage at Staveley and Darnall depots. The apparently open landscape east of Woodhouse, near the former Midland viaduct, is the location of this view which lends a certain license that the D11 could be doing 70 plus along the GC main with a Marylebone express circa 1925 - if only! Withdrawn in August 1960, No.62669 was hauled off to Doncaster works for scrapping that same month. *(BLP - E310)*

(opposite) In October 1956 the Gresley A8 class was fully intact and Middlesbrough based No.69854, seen here on Darlington shed yard, had just undergone a 'General' repair at Darlington works. That visit was its last prior to returning to be condemned and cut up in May 1960. Rebuilt by Gresley during the 1930's from the North Eastern 4-4-4 Class H tank engines, the A8 turned out to be superior in Pacific profile compared to their earlier guise. As a class, the forty-five A8's could be found working all over the former territory of the North Eastern. No.69854, rebuilt in 1933, had done the rounds since then and had been allocated to Whitby, Neville Hill, Darlington, West Auckland, Hull Botanic Gardens, and from September 1957 to Sunderland - virtually every corner of the old NER in Yorkshire and County Durham. The A8 class was, it appears, prone to colliding with anything because the Engine History Cards recount twenty-two instances of collision including one with an aircraft at Dinsdale in 1943. As 4-4-4's they seemed to be much better behaved as only one derailment is recorded. *(BLP - E339)*

Retford ex-GC shed (Thrumpton) had few mixed traffic or passenger locomotives compared with the ex Great Northern establishment on the other side of the ECML. Thompson B1 No.61208 was one of the few and the shed had gained its services immediately after the locomotive was handed over to the LNER in July 1947 by NBL Co. Always kept in a clean condition and well looked after, the engine is seen outside the shed in February 1959. When the ex-GC shed was closed in early 1965 the B1 moved to the ex-GN shed but when that place closed in the summer of 65', the engine moved to Doncaster albeit for a short time because on 26th September it was condemned and two months after that sold for scrap to T.W.Ward at Beighton. During its eighteen year life, the locomotive had undergone six 'General' repairs, five at Doncaster and one at Stratford, and one 'non-classified' repair. *(BLP - E337)*

With a stiff westerly breeze blowing, immaculate A4 No.60028 WALTER K.WHIGHAM climbs Gamston curve with an Up afternoon express in October 1958. Now with a double chimney, the locomotive had not been near works for a year yet it still looks pristine - of course it will be no surprise to learn that it was a King's Cross Pacific. During its lifetime, from new in March 1937, this engine had no less than seven different liveries: Green as new; Garter blue from February 1938; Unlined black from November 1941; Garter blue again from October 1947; BR's trial purple from June 1948; Dark blue from October 1950 and finally, Brunswick green from February 1952. Condemned in December 1962, it entered Doncaster works for scrapping during the following January. *(BLP - E340)*

New England V2 No.60820 has charge of a southbound local passenger train in May 1961 and is climbing Gamston bank with no apparent effort. Looking less than pristine, the twenty-four years old V2 had one more repair, a 'Casual Light' carried out at Darlington in September 1961, before withdrawal in June 1962. It entered Doncaster works for scrapping on Wednesday 20th June 1962 and was broken up shortly afterwards. Although spending most of its life at former Great Northern sheds on the ECML, this V2 had two three-year stints working from Woodford Halse and Leicester sheds on the ex GCR main line, followed by another year at Neasden depot. *(BLP - E940)*

E4 No.62785 at Mildenhall this time. It is still May 1958 and the 2-4-0 has the late afternoon train to Fordham Junction and then on to Cambridge. This is certainly a typical pre-Beeching branch line scene which, although gone forever, still holds a great deal of charm. *(BLP - E935)*

South Blyth based J27 No.65882 had just finished a 'General' overhaul at Darlington works when Keith Pirt copped it on the yard at Darlington shed on Thursday 14th May 1964. During the 'running-in' trials undertaken by all ex-works locomotives, the J27 was found to require further attention and returned to works on Tuesday 26th but after minor adjustments it left Darlington on Friday 29th (the engine's last works visit). At the end of April 1967 the 0-6-0 transferred to Sunderland shed to join the diminishing band of active North Eastern Region steam. On 9th September it was condemned along with all the other able bodied steam locomotives and in October was sold to the T.J.Thompson scrapyard at Stockton. *(BLP - E929)*

Making its way home after a 'General' (13th February to 17th March) at Darlington works, New England V2 No.60867 charges past Retford South signal box with an Up express in late March 1959. The electrical apparatus for the Automatic Train Control system had been fitted during the overhaul and now the locomotive was fully equipped after the mechanical parts had been fitted at an earlier works visit in August 1958. Built in July 1939, No.60867 was one of the V2's which worked throughout WWII and helped the class gain the reputation for which they became well known. It was allocated to Doncaster shed up to the end of August 1955 when it went south to New England. One of the early withdrawal casualties, 60867 was condemned on 1st May 1962 and was cut up at Doncaster works during the same month. (BLP - E373)

The morning Cleethorpes to King's Cross express was usually a 'Britannia' working in 1961 but a failure could find one of Immingham's Thompson B1's taking the train to London as was the case on this August morning in 1961 when No.61190 deputised. 'Brit's' 70039, 70040 and 70041 were at Immingham depot at the time and they were later joined by 70035, 70036, 70037 and 70038 in the October. Seen on the ECML south of Hatfield, the fairly clean B1 is going well on the Up fast line. Built by NB Loco. in May 1947, the engine spent the first three years of its life working from Doncaster shed but in June 1950 it moved to Immingham for a fifteen year stay. When the Humberside shed was dieselised in 1965 the B1 moved over to Canklow and on 13th June it was reallocated to Colwick, however, No.61190 probably never went to the Nottingham shed because on the 20th June it was condemned and then in August it was sold to scrap merchant T.W.Ward who cut up the engine at their Beighton yard. *(BLP - E371)*

The first of A.J.Hill's last class of GER 0-6-0's, the D81 (LNER Class J20), had been built before Stratford had completed the building of his penultimate GER 0-6-0 design the 177 class (LNER Class J19). Being fairly young for pre-Grouping engines, the whole class, which was eventually to number thirty-five saw service into the late 1950's and into the early years of the next decade. No.64672 was built at Stratford in October 1920 and did not quite make it to its fortieth birthday, before being withdrawn on the first day of 1959. Here at March station in May 1958 it is having any easy time on the apparent run down to condemnation, however, it did visit works from 24th September to 10th October for a 'Casual Light' repair. March shed, where the engine had been stationed since reallocating on 2nd March 1952, seems to have looked after the J19, at least externally, and it presents a tidy picture here. Originally only twenty-five J19's were constructed but during the 1930's the LNER rebuilt the ten 1912-built engines making up the J18 class to J19 standard. *(BLP - E329)*

The former LMS engine shed at Perth was one of those provided with a large mechanical coaling plant which could in fact refill the tenders of four locomotives simultaneously. However, the plant was rarely, if ever called upon to perform such a feat and certainly by September 1964 its working day was getting shorter by the week as the depot's own fleet of steam locomotives was diminishing slowly and the number of visiting steam locomotives was also becoming less. A4 No.60023 GOLDEN EAGLE has just topped-up its tender after working into Perth with an afternoon fish train from Aberdeen which was handed over to one of the few remaining ex-LMS Coronation Pacific's still active at this time, for the run to London. No.60023 is turned ready to work back northwards but within weeks it would be condemned and sold for scrap to the same yard as No.60006. *(BLP E350)*

En route, probably to Scunthorpe, Thompson O1 No.63795 drifts towards the GC/GN level crossing at Retford with a heavy coke train from Sheffield in October 1963. The Staveley based O1 had certainly been around the former LNER lines since it was rebuilt from an O4 Part 3 at Gorton in early 1944. Its first shed after release from the 'shops' was West Hartlepool from where a month later it reallocated to Gorton shed. Some six years in Manchester passed by before its next move took it to Annesley in April 1950. The Nottinghamshire depot became something of a 'spiritual home' for this class with dozens of them concentrated there throughout BR days. When the BR Standard 9F's started to infiltrate the GC main line freight workings, some of the Annesley O1's moved away to March and No.63795 was one of them, arriving in Cambridgeshire in February 1957. After nearly three years hauling coal and fast freight over the main lines of the Fens, this O1 came back to the East Midlands and settled in at the former Great Central shed at Staveley. The haulage of coal and its various derivatives was the business of the railways in the Nottinghamshire and Derbyshire coalfield, as in any other, and so 63795 carried on the tradition until condemned in October 1963. The O1 was sent to Doncaster for scrapping in February 1964 exactly twenty years since its emergence from Gorton works as one of Thompson's new 'standard' heavy freight engines. In the right background can be seen the water softening plant at the old Great Northern engine shed. *(BLP - E308)*

Like all the major locomotive works, Doncaster required the use of a number of shunting locomotives to move the 'dead' engines around the place, shunt wagon loads of stores and spare parts etc., also the wagons of scrap which built up. J52 No.68784 was one of the 'Plant' shunters in May 1956 and though it was attached to the works on a permanent basis, it was actually allocated to Doncaster shed - 36A. Built by Neilson & Co. in July 1896, as Great Northern Railway No.1047, it was classified by the LNER at Grouping as J53. But not for long because in November 1923 it went into Doncaster works for a 'General' overhaul and was rebuilt to J52 standard at the same time. At the time it was working from Hornsey shed and continued to do so until September 1952 when it transferred to Doncaster engine shed. Although maintained by Doncaster works until near the end of WWII, in May 1945 it went to Stratford works for the first of two 'Generals', a 'Light' and a 'Casual Light' carried out there. In 1953 and by now a 'local' engine, it reverted to Doncaster maintenance although it was only to receive a 'General' in January 1953 which became its last repair. When it entered the works for shunting purposes is not known but normally once an engine got onto the workforce it usually never returned to normal traffic again. And that was the case with No.68784 because in November 1957, in dire need of attention, it was condemned and cut up within days. *(BLP - E941)*

King's Cross A3 No.60062 MINORU takes a diverted Up Sunday express through the cutting south of Gainsborough (Lea Road) station in April 1961. One of the A3's rebuilt from the original Gresley A1's, 60062 went back into traffic shortly after D-Day 1944 being allocated to New England shed for a couple of weeks before moving to Gorton shed in Manchester for a four month stint working on the old Great Central main line. After that it went back to the Great Northern for the first of three periods of allocation to King's Cross shed. This engine certainly got around during its twenty years as an A3 because shortly before the end of W.W.II it was shedded at Edinburgh Haymarket for six weeks prior to returning to Top shed. At the end of May 1948, whilst numbered E62 it moved to Leeds Copley Hill for three years but moved away from there with the arrival of the Peppercorn A1's. Doncaster was its next shed followed by Grantham in February 1953 and then in the October of that year it went to King's Cross for an eight year stay where its external appearance during that time, as seen here, was a credit to the staff at the London depot. In September 1961, with diesel motive power taking over the express passenger trains on the ECML, 60062 went to New England shed then, in June 1963 to Grantham followed by Doncaster three months later. Miraculously, the A3 was kept working and six weeks later moved back to New England where it found work until condemned on Boxing Day 1964, one of the last of the A3's. The engine was sold privately for scrap and moved to R.A.King's yard at Norwich in 1965, some forty years after it had emerged from Doncaster works as one of the infant LNER's new A1 Pacific's. *(BLP - E344)*

Keith Pirt described this picture as "...a classic, beautiful slide..." We obviously agree. The locomotive is Peppercorn A2 No.60530 SAYAJIRAO. The train is an evening Glasgow to Dundee express in September 1965. The location is Kinbuck bank with the reflection in Allanwater. *(BLP - E400)*

Doncaster based Peppercorn A1 No.60128 BONGRACE rushing a King's Cross bound express past Barrowby Road junction in April 1963. By this period most of the express passenger trains on the ECML were in the hands of diesel locomotives with the Deltics handling the most important trains. No.60128 was probably deputising for a failure of which there were many during those early days of dieselisation. Hanging on at Doncaster until the end of 1964, BONGRACE was condemned on 10th January 1965 and sold the following month to Draper's. *(BLP - E915)*

Gateshead A4 No.60005 SIR CHARLES NEWTON turns on Haymarket turntable in May 1959 after working into Edinburgh (Waverley) with an express from Newcastle. One of the final trio of A4 which entered traffic in 1938, 60005 was built with a double chimney. Named CAPERCAILLIE until July 1942, the engine had been renamed CHARLES H.NEWTON, after the LNER's Chief General Manager, when it came out of Doncaster 'Plant' on 19th August. At the same time its side skirting had been removed to allow for easier maintenance but the original blue livery had been replaced by black paint under the wartime economy measures. The SIR was added to the nameplate in June 1943 after Charles Newton became a Knight. Being based at Gateshead for most of its life, this A4 had no need for a corridor tender and actually kept the same streamlined tender (No.5641) from entry to traffic until it was sold for scrap in June 1964. Ousted from ECML workings in late 1963, No.60005 went to St Margarets for a couple of weeks before moving northwards to Aberdeen Ferryhill and a new though short lease of life on the Glasgow expresses. It was condemned 12th March 1964 and cut up at G.H.Campbell's Airdrie yard later that summer. (BLP - E368)

Now and again a particular type of picture can bring back memories so strong it is as though it was only yesterday when you last saw that scene in reality. This is one of those images. York Leeman Road engine shed, October 1964. V2 No.60895, Peppercorn K1 No.62061 and some B1's. Smoke, steam, sun, shadows, working engines at rest. KRP described this picture simply as "...magic!". We agree totally. *(BLP - E925)*

I think this is the first Heaton based locomotive featured in this album, certainly the first 'Geordie' V2. No.60846 was one of the 'separate cylinder' V2's and in October 1959 it is seen leaving York and passing Leeman Road engine shed with a Down express for Newcastle. By now this engine was fully equipped with ATC having had the electrical apparatus fitted at a 'General' undertaken during the previous July. One of the 1939 batch of V2's, No.60846 spent its first twelve years working from Doncaster shed after which it went to Copley Hill for a twenty-one month stint. Ardsley shed got it in June 1953 and kept hold of the 2-6-2 until September 1958 when it moved north to Heaton. Less than two years were spent on the north bank of the Tyne before 60846 went to the recently opened engine shed at Thornaby. During its time on Tees-side the V2 managed to get in no less than eight visits to Darlington works including a 'General', three 'Casual Light' and four 'Non-classified' repairs. Miraculously it was not condemned during a period when most steam locomotives which entered those works never came out again intact. A transfer to St Margarets shed, at the end of February 1963, secured even more time for 60846 and it carried on working until October 1965 when circumstances caught up with it at last. The V2 was sold for scrap in December to G.H.Campbell at Airdrie. *(BLP - E916)*

Just two months before it was withdrawn, Selby based D20 No.62387 was called upon to head a special from Leeds to Scarborough in June 1957. Here, with the immaculate exNER 4-4-0 in charge, the train has called at York Holgate on the outward journey. Note the rebuilt NER tender, one of ten such D20 tenders which had new straight sided bodies, similar to the LNER Group Standard tender, fitted on the existing chassis; NER type buffers were retained. No.62387 had this tender (ex 62386) from April 1954 until withdrawal. Shortly after this special working, No.62387 was reallocated to Alnmouth shed where it was condemned 2nd September 1957, just over fifty years old. The last six D20's all gravitated to Alnmouth in 1957 prior to withdrawal. *(BLP - E362)*

A4 No.60029 (LNER No.4493) WOODCOCK was the second member of the class to carry that name from new. No.4489 (60010) carried the name for two weeks whilst running trials on the ECML prior to receiving its Garter blue livery and becoming one of the five A4's chosen to work the *CORONATION* train. After return to the works the nameplate was removed and then on 15th June No.4489 was named DOMINION OF CANADA. Meanwhile A4 No.4493 was nearing completion at Doncaster and it was next in line for naming. With the five 'non-stop' engines now into traffic, the works could concentrate on the next batch of A4's which would be turned out in green livery. No.4493 was put into traffic at the end of July 1937 wearing green paint and carrying the name WOODCOCK. Initially allocated to Gateshead shed, the A4 had little chance of working the 'glamour' trains unless one of the rostered engines failed. However, a move to King's Cross shed in February 1938 and then a change of livery to Garter blue during a 'shopping' in the following July meant the engine became a regular on the *CORONATION* from thereon; at least to the start of WWII. A 'Top shed' engine for most of its life, No.60029 moved to New England when 34A closed but did little work from there and in October 1963 it was condemned. Lying derelict over the next few months, it entered Doncaster works on 4th January 1964 for scrapping. In this May 1960 view at Grantham shed, the A4 was, as usual for a 34A Pacific, looking immaculate. *(BLP - E903)*

After spending most of its life working from Edinburgh area sheds, including the ex Caledonian engine shed at Dalry Road (May 1951 to October 1952), J37 No.64547 left for Dundee at the end of March 1964. In June 1965, not long after completing a 'Light Intermediate' repair at Inverurie works, the 0-6-0 was on the Tayport goods run and is seen at Wormit station awaiting a signal. Built at Cowlairs in November 1915, the J37 was repaired exclusively at Cowlairs until the beginning of the BR era when, from June 1951, it then travelled to Inverurie for 'shopping'. The Dundee reallocation gave the engine a further extension of work but in this period of the 1960's the life of any steam locomotive was precarious and on the last day of 1966 No.64547 was condemned and three months later it was in the hands of scrap merchant J.McWilliam at Shettleston. *(BLP - E397)*

Copley Hill Peppercorn A1 No.60131 OSPREY, heads the Up *YORKSHIRE PULLMAN* through Gamston curve on a crisp morning in October 1957. Resident in Leeds from February 1953, No.60131 went to Ardsley shed in April 1962 as the big diesels started to take over on services such as this. The Pacific returned to Leeds at the end of July 1963 but to Neville Hill shed from where it worked for two more years or so before being condemned in October 1965. It was sold for scrap to T.W.Ward at Killamarsh. *(BLP - E928)*

(opposite) O4/8 No.63655 basks in the sun outside Retford Thrumpton shed on a March Sunday in 1959. This former Ministry of Munitions (No.1616), Kitson built, Robinson 2-8-0 was purchased by the LNER in 1923 and after undergoing a thorough overhaul entered traffic at Gorton shed on 15th February 1924 as No.6364. Within a week it was sent to Immingham shed from where it worked up to April 1930 whence it reallocated to March shed. After five years on the Fens it moved to Cambridge for three months then returned to March depot for a six year residence. In October 1941 and six months after being rebuilt to a Part 7 engine, No.6364 went to more familiar territory, allocated to Barnsley shed where for two years it helped move the vast amounts of coal produced in that particular area of Yorkshire. At the end of August 1943, with the build-up of Operation Overlord gaining momentum, the O4 was sent to the twelve road shed at Staveley on the exGC main line. On the 8th August of the following year it transferred to Woodford on the 'Extension' from where it saw the end of hostilities. Frodingham depot at Scunthorpe got the engine in early 1946 when it was fresh from a 'General' overhaul at Gorton works. Retford shed and the Nottinghamshire coalfield beckoned in January 1955 and two years later it went into Gorton for rebuilding to a Part 8 engine. Returning to Retford shed, it worked out the rest of its life on coal trains until displaced by diesel motive power in December 1962. Condemnation came on the 29th of that month, a relatively early demise for a Part 8 O4. After lying rusting at Retford shed for nine months or so it was towed to Doncaster works in August 1963 for scrapping. *(BLP - E383)*

In March 1962 at Markham Moor, Thompson A2/3 No.60516 HYCILLA has charge of the Sundays Only Grantham to Doncaster 'Parly' stopping train. Working its way home, the York based A2/3 had spent much of its short life working from Tyneside sheds until its June 1960 move to York shed for its final months of work. Although withdrawn in December 1962, the locomotive had done little work since the cessation of the Summer timetable in September. It entered Doncaster works for scrapping on April Fool's day 1963. *(BLP - E360)*

(opposite) G5 No.67340 was unique amongst the 110 strong class by dint of its extended side tanks. The extensions had been fitted during a General overhaul at Darlington which lasted from 3rd December 1937 to 15th March 1938, and were into to give the engine an extra 220 gallons water capacity so that it could be tried against railcars on the Hull-Pontefract and the Hull-York routes. For the trial period the G5 was loaned by Sunderland, its home shed then, to Hull Botanic Gardens shed for the period 20th March to 20th June 1938. In the event the trials were not a success for the 0-4-4T and it was then drafted to South Blyth shed, keeping the tank extensions for the rest of its life. On 27th February 1939 it emerged from works having been fitted with vacuum operated push & pull gear and afterwards moved south to Starbeck shed. On 29th April 1942 it went back to Botanic Gardens shed for a somewhat longer stay than previously taken. On 21st November 1954 No.67340 moved back north to South Blyth and is seen outside the shed in this March 1957 view. Built as North Eastern Railway No.387, both Gateshead and Darlington workshops maintained this engine during its fifty-seven year existence, the latter works scrapping it in April 1958. *(BLP - E369)*

Amongst the last of its class to be built, Thompson B1 No.61402 was one of the Darlington batch and came into traffic on 27th April 1950. It was allocated to Kittybrewster shed in Aberdeen initially but in July in transferred to Dundee Tay Bridge shed. The engine worked in Scotland for the whole of its short life and was maintained by Cowlairs works, although it is recorded that Inverurie carried a couple of minor repairs in 1963. This view shows the engine in late June 1959 outside Eastfield shed when it had just completed a five-week long 'Non-classified' repair when AWS had been fitted. Prior to that No.61402 had finished a 'General' which had only taken three weeks - obviously some parts of the AWS apparatus must have been in short supply. The clean paintwork gives away the fact that 'General' had been carried out in recent weeks and its time out of traffic during the N/C repair obviously helped keep it fairly clean this long. Note the footplate lining has been completed in the Cowlairs style with curves rather than angles, as was the norm at other works. The B1 was withdrawn in June 1964 and was sold two months later for scrap. *(BLP - E387)*

Passing High Dyke sidings and about to enter Stoke tunnel, A3 No.60111 ENTERPRISE has charge of an Up express in August 1962. This Grantham based double chimney engine had been fitted with the German type trough smoke deflectors at a 'Casual Light' repair (its last) in April. Rebuilt from an A1 as early as July 1927, No.60111 would be condemned at the end of 1962 and enter Doncaster works for scrapping in April 1963. *(BLP - E909)*

July 1961 and the ECML was still a stronghold (just) for steam and in this morning view of Grantham based O2 No.63933 heading south for home and just passing under Eaton wood road bridge with a heavy freight, we can see two sludge carriers coupled next to the engine. Comprised from the withdrawn locomotive tender stock, the sludge carrier fleet on the former LNER lines numbered dozens of units made up from various pre-Group types. They even had their own number group (SC XXXX) in the Departmental rolling stock fleet. Necessary to store and transport the sludge created at the water softening plants located around the Eastern Region, the SC's were run to and from their intended locations in ordinary goods trains such as this. The sludge generated was usually hauled to Doncaster where a number of tenders were then made up into their own train for a trip to one of the various special tips used for the purpose of disposing the sludge. These two SC's were most probably be bound for Grantham shed which had its own water softening plant. The O2 still had nearly eighteen months work in front of it before withdrawal in December 1962. It was later sold for scrap to the Central Wagon Co., in Wigan. *(BLP - E352)*

During its second residency at Fort William shed, J36 No.65313 is caught on camera in July 1959 as it shunts the Mallaig line observation coach and three other carriages at Fort William. Having spent much of its life working in the Glasgow area, the J36 first came to Fort William in September 1945. After two years by the sea it went back to the industrial belt and Polmont shed in October 1947. On 4th January 1948, still as LNER No.5313, it steamed off to Fort William again but this time for a thirteen year 'holiday' as seen here. Eastfield shed called it in at the end of February 1961 but the little 0-6-0 escaped to Fort William six days later, determined no doubt to complete a third 'tour' and end its days there. The J36 managed to achieve both of those ambitions and was finally withdrawn on 30th July 1962, at the age of 63 years. Inverurie had been its maintenance base since the 1920's and it was broken up there in October 1962. Note the K1 in the background handling fish empties. *(BLP - E948)*

This view of K3 No.61921 on Retford GC shed yard in June 1961 was taken just weeks before the engine was condemned and then cut up at Doncaster works. During the great massacre of the Gresley 2-6-0s in the early years of the 1960's. Built by Armstrong Whitworth in July 1934 bearing the LNER number 1308, this K3 spent its first eight years of life working on the North Eastern Area at both Heaton and Tweedmouth sheds. In March 1942 it was transferred to the Great Eastern section and until withdrawal, it was allocated to six different sheds ranging from March to Yarmouth. This visit to Retford was captured probably when the engine was on its final journey, en route to Doncaster. *(BLP - E722)*

Just weeks after completing its last 'General' repair at Gorton works, Langwith Junction based J11/3 No.64332 rests on Retford in November 1960. Note the new BR crest on the tender. This engine did in fact reallocate to Retford shed during the following January, its last shed move in many. Condemned 23rd September 1962, No.64332 was cut up at Gorton shortly afterward. Besides spending most of its fifty-nine year life at depots on or near its native GCR network, the J11 also had a couple of stints on completely foreign ground. In October 1928, when it was a Leicester based engine, it was sent to Norwich for three months where a number of the class were already working. On its return it went to more familiar territory at Colwick. Then, in July 1939, it went to Melton Constable shed on the M&GN for three months. In all this engine had fifteen shed reallocations although not all to different establishments - Colwick had it four times, Leicester for the same number, Retford twice, Annesley, Gorton and Langwith each had the engine once, Gorton for some twelve years from April 1943. *(BLP - E357)*

Looking at this picture of Peppercorn A1 No.60115 MEG MERRILIES standing at the head of a northbound train in the Down Nottingham platform of Grantham station in September 1962, it seems incredible that the locomotive was only two months away from withdrawal. However, that was the case for this fourteen years old Copley Hill based engine which was one of half a dozen of the class condemned in that last quarter of 1962. No.60115 entered Doncaster works for the last time at the end of May 1963 after six months laid up at Copley Hill, ousted from its regular duties by the recently delivered fleet of 'Deltic' diesel locomotives. *(BLP - E359)*

(opposite) Although it was not intended to include preserved steam within this album, we thought that this pleasing view of K1 No.2005 leaving Whitby in June 1975 with the first steam train in ten years, albeit a NYMR special to Pickering, was just the ticket. *(BLP - E367)*

Parkeston based Thompson B1 No.61384 approaches Retford level crossing with a Sheffield bound train in March 1959. Keith Pirt states that the locomotive is "...ex-works..." but the B1 had been ex Stratford on the previous 28th November, some four months past. So, either the Engine History Card is incorrect or KRP has his dates mixed up. One other theory is that Parkeston shed kept this engine immaculately clean for some reason which 'bucks the trend' of the period. If any reader knows the answer to any of these three probable's with any certainty, the Publisher would like to hear from them. For the record, the train seems to be the nameless *NORTH COUNTRY CONTINENTAL*, due through Retford at about midday during 1959. The B1 may well have been standing in for a 'Britannia', the more usual motive power for this train between Parkeston and Sheffield. No.61384 was one of the North British Loco. Co. built engines which came into traffic in October 1951 working firstly from Ardsley then Bradford Hammerton Street before moving to the former G.E. Section in October 1952. In September 1956 it was allocated to Parkeston and then in April 1960 it came back north as far as Lincoln. All through the period it spent on the former Great Eastern, it was maintained by Stratford works. Withdrawn from Immingham in October 1965, 61384 was sold to a private scrap merchant in February 1966. *(BLP - E361)*

Having just returned to March shed after a five month spell at King's Lynn, B17 No.61626 BRANCEPETH CASTLE looks worn out even in the spring sunshine of April 1959. After a near thirty year long career which kept it tied to engine sheds situated on the former Great Eastern system, this engine still had another reallocation to do before being condemned at Doncaster works in January 1960. Its last shed was Cambridge where it had once spent four days in March 1940. It did not spend much longer there on its last trip and after arriving on 6th December 1959 it was sent north to 'The Plant' shortly after New Years Day 1960, never to return. Four different workshops looked after this particular locomotive during its lifetime: Darlington, Doncaster, Gorton and Stratford all gave it 'Generals' at one time or another and not in any order, as was the case with many other B17's. *(BLP - E382)*

Relegated to working traffic which was previously the preserve of Gresley's K2 and K3 class engines, A3 No.60108 GAY CRUSADER heads a King's Cross bound parcels train along the slow line south of Hatfield in May 1961. The Top shed A3 had been allocated to King's Cross no less than six times since it was rebuilt from an A1 in January 1943. In between those times it had also done three stints at Neasden and two more working from Doncaster shed. However, it was not finished yet by any means as it still had another two and half years of life in front of it and three more depots would host it in that period. Strangely, the sequence of sheds each took it further north to meet the scrapmen. In September 1961 it transferred to New England and worked from there until June 1963 when Grantham took it in for three months. Then it was Doncaster's turn but only briefly because six weeks later on 19th October 1963 it was condemned having just passed its fortieth birthday. I suppose it would have been appropriate to have sent it into Doncaster works for cutting up because the engine had been built and always maintained there but sentiment was in short supply on BR during the 1960's. No.60108 was sent to Darlington and entered those works on 16th November 1963. *(BLP - E311)*

Running light engine on the ex GC line near Ordsall, Retford, in March 1961, O2 No.63939 presents a nice picture for an engine nearly forty years old, however, it had not long been out of Doncaster works after its last overhaul. Built in December 1923, the engine could lay claim to be LNER vintage but its origins went back to 1918 when the class first appeared. For its first twenty years No.63939 worked from New England shed hauling coal trains to London and empties back. It moved to Doncaster on 10th December 1943 but the following month it joined the hordes of other O2's which swamped Colwick shed during the latter stages of WWII. After exactly a year at Colwick the engine returned to New England but after less than six months there it went to Grantham until February 1947 when Frodingham shed called. It stayed at Scunthorpe for nearly eight years after which it did six years at Doncaster prior to its January 1960 allocation to Retford. Like many of the O2's, this 2-8-0 was withdrawn in September 1963 and sold for scrap - 63939 went to a Nottingham breaker. *(BLP - E377)*

It has been mentioned elsewhere in this album that King's Cross shed had a reputation in BR days for keeping its main line locomotives in a superb external condition whereas Gateshead shed basically achieved the opposite in that their charges were mechanically sound enough but cleaning was not one of the depot's priorities. As if to prove the point, A4 No.60002 SIR MURROUGH WILSON comes into view at Markham Moor summit with an afternoon King's Cross to Newcastle express in March 1961 looking lass than resplendent with an appearance which was hardly expected for a top link locomotive on the ECML. Except for a six week stint at King's Cross shed in 1943, this A4 had spent all of its life allocated to Gateshead shed from new in April 1938 to withdrawal in May 1964. It even kept the same tender (No.5673) which was one of the non-corridor streamlined type. Like the other A4's, No.60002 was always maintained at Doncaster but two entries on its History Card show it to have had non-classified repairs at Gateshead works in March 1955 which, given the geographical proximity of the works to the running shed is understandable to sort out some minor problem which was beyond the capability of the shed fitters'. However, the other entry shows that the engine visited Cowlairs works on Saturday 20th September 1947 just for that day. Whatever the reason, the engine had obviously worked into Glasgow and require some immediate attention prior to its return working. This engine was one of the few A4's which were sold to private scrap merchants and it ended up in the yard of G.Cohen at Cargo Fleet just a few months after being condemned. *(BLP - E313)*

In October 1959 the former Great Central C13's were coming to the end of their lives. No.67417, seen here in store at Gorton shed, was already fifty-six years old and was looking every one of those years. Three months from the date of this exposure and the 4-4-2T would be condemned and then cut up at the adjacent works with neither ceremony or fanfare. The engine had done the job it was designed for so, there was nothing special about this particular locomotive other than it had certainly served its masters. It was also the last of the C13 class. The last of the similar C14 class, No.67450, was also condemned on the same day, at the same venue. With that event two locomotive classes became extinct but also disappearing forever were the Great Central examples of the 4-4-2 Atlantic wheelbase. *(BLP - 943)*

B16 No.61425 had just returned to Neville Hill shed from a 'Casual Light' repair at Darlington works when KRP took this view on 29th March 1958. This reliable and hard working class of seventy 4-6-0's were used on mixed traffic duties and during the forty-odd year existence of the class they were allocated mainly within the boundaries of the old North Eastern Railway. Except for a period during WWII, when all the class were concentrated at York shed, Neville Hill shed had been associated with the B16's since their introduction in 1919. The first of the class to be condemned (apart from No.925 in 1942) was No.61474 in January 1958 but it was later the following year before any more went. No.61425 was withdrawn at the end of the summer timetable in 1961 and cut up at Darlington in November. *(BLP - E316)*

Winter photography can be a bit hit and miss, at least it used to be prior to the digital revolution. However, when the sun shone and the right subject appeared in the viewfinder, it was worth getting the cold feet along with the other non-feeling extremities which reminded you that it might be sensible to be indoors. Braving the cold in November 1962, KRP captured this lovely scene for us of A3 No.60070 GLADIATEUR on the climb to Markham Moor with an Up parcels train. The exhaust, described as 'woolly', looks superb as the A3 digs in for the summit. Ardsley based No.60070, one of the Gresley A10 engines rebuilt to A3 standard, was put back into traffic in January 1947 at Gateshead shed. It ended its career at the same shed in May 1964 but only after fifteen other reallocations in between time. The latter shed moves included one to Holbeck shed in Leeds from where, during the winter of 1960-61 it helped out over the Settle & Carlisle line with the Anglo-Scottish expresses. The trough type smoke deflectors were fitted during a 'General' in 1961 and to some those fittings were advantageous to the looks of the A3's. Being a late withdrawal, in May 1964, No.60070 was sold to a private scrap merchant and it was cut up in Hull later that year. *(BLP - E322)*

St Margarets based V2 No.60816 starts away from Perth with a morning Dundee to Glasgow train in June 1964. Although this engine had spent all of its life allocated to just three Scottish sheds - Aberdeen (3 times), Haymarket (4 times) and St Margarets (4 times), it had been maintained by four different ex LNER workshops - Darlington, Doncaster, Cowlairs and Inverurie, the latter only commanding one visit and that during wartime. Cowlairs managed about four visits from the locomotive and those for only light or non-classified repairs lasting just a few days. The engine's main repair base, and its birthplace, was Darlington (after 1st August 1943) and its last 'General' was completed there at the end of September 1963. Condemned in October 1965, No.60816 was sold for scrap the following December. *(BLP - E307)*

Ready to depart Grantham station with an Up express in May 1959, Doncaster based A3 No.60112 ST SIMON had just come out of Doncaster works after receiving a 'Non-classified' repair. In October 1962 the trough type smoke deflectors were fitted. Rebuilt from an A10 in August 1946, this engine had a total working life of just over forty-one years with all but five months of that time allocated to ex Great Northern depots. As LNER No.4481, the engine was named in October 1925 after the 1884 Ascot Gold Cup winner. Condemned on Boxing Day 1964 it was sold for scrap to R.A.King of Norwich in February 1965. *(BLP - E386)*

Exiting the north end of Perth (General) on a June evening in 1964, A4 No.60010 DOMINION OF CANADA has charge of the evening Glasgow to Aberdeen express. This is the work for which these streamliners were basically saved from the scrapheap and what a good job they did in the short time of their involvement. Luckily a number made it to preservation of one kind or another just by being at Ferryhill shed for these duties. Destined eventually for preservation in Canada, No.60010 was withdrawn at Darlington works at the end of May 1965. However, it was then put into open storage at Bank Top engine shed until August 1966 when it was towed to Crewe works for external restoration prior to being shipped across the Atlantic. *(BLP - E324)*

One of the Great Central built 2-8-0's, O4 Part 8 No.63914 had started life at Gorton works in October 1919 as a Class 8M engine which had a larger diameter boiler than the 8K class (LNER O4) engines. Because of the 5ft 6in. diameter boiler the LNER had to classify the 8M as Class O5. However, trying its best to standardise in any way it could, the LNER decided to rebuild the O5's to O4 standard and 63914, then numbered LNER 5012, was the first to be 'shopped'. On emergence from Gorton in August 1926, it looked essentially like an O4 Part 1 but it retained the wide cab of the O5 albeit with a new frontplate. Later on, in line with the other rebuilt O5's, they were reclassified O4 Part 6. But for the last two years, when it reallocated to Retford shed, this engine spent the whole of its LNER career at Mexborough shed working coal trains. Its new home provided much the same kind of duties albeit in a less steeply graded landscape. In May 1955 it entered Gorton works for a 'General' and came out at the end of July rebuilt to O4 Part 8 standard having regained a 5ft 6in. diameter boiler but of the Thompson (Diagram 100A) kind. All together ninety-nine O4's were rebuilt to Part 8 standard up to 1958 when the rebuilding programme was halted by the London Midland Region who had then taken over Gorton works from the Eastern Region. Perhaps the rest of the O4 fleet would have been dealt with if things had been different. Anyway in this June 1961 view of No.63914 outside Retford Thrumpton ex-GC shed, the engine is looking fairly clean having recently returned from a 'Heavy Intermediate' at Gorton. Not one of the last of the Part 8 engines to go, 63914 was condemned 28th May 1964 and sold in August to a private scrapyard in Nottingham. Thrumpton shed closed in January 1965. (BLP - E323)

Having spent eleven years working over former Great Eastern lines from the March and Stratford depots, Peppercorn K1 No.62015 joined the stud of locomotives at Retford engine shed towards the end of September 1961 shortly after completing a 'General' overhaul at Doncaster works. One year later Keith Pirt caught it on camera in the yard of the exGC shed and considering it had been busy on all sorts of jobs from coal haulage to parcels and passenger train working, its appearance was quite respectable. By November it would be transferred to Doncaster shed and after two years there Frodingham shed called in January 1965, no doubt iron ore haulage would be another of the K1's tricks during the six month residency amongst the steel works. Two weeks after its sixteenth birthday, No.62015 was withdrawn and on 8th November 1965 it was cut up at Draper's scrapyard in Hull. *(BLP - E309)*

(opposite) Up to March 1963, Thompson B1 No.61152 had spent most of its short life working from Sheffield area sheds and here in May 1958, when allocated to Darnall shed, it is making a somewhat spirited exit from platform 4 at Sheffield (Victoria) with an Up express. One of the Vulcan Foundry, Newton-le-Willows, Lancashire, built B1's, (6)1152 entered traffic along with (6)1153 on Friday 2nd May 1947 at Gorton shed where it was tested out before being allocated to Darnall shed on 4th June, also with No.1153. Until early 1953 it was maintained by Gorton works but thereafter Darlington took over until 1959 when Doncaster started to look after it. The B1 became 61152 on 15th January 1949 after completing a 'General' at Gorton. For seven weeks during the autumn of 1957, the B1 was sent to Doncaster shed but returned to Darnall on 17th November. Two years later an unusual allocation took it to the former Midland shed at Millhouses for a seventeen month stay after which it returned once again to Darnall. Shortly before Darnall shed banished steam for ever, No.61152 moved to Immingham where, in April 1964, it was condemned. By some quirk of fate, the B1 was sold two months later for scrap to the Central Wagon Co., at Ince, Wigan, Lancashire - the same county where, seventeen years previously, it was built. *(BLP - E320)*

O2 No.63936 stands in the June sunshine of 1962 at Thrumpton engine shed Retford during the engines last full year of operation. The O2 had arrived at Retford exactly one year before from Grantham shed where it had been stationed since the end of hostilities in 1945. To help keep it going during its time at Retford, the 2-8-0 was given a 'General' overhaul at Doncaster which unusually took over eight weeks to complete (4th October to 5th December 1961). That repair was 63936's last. Three months short of its fortieth birthday, the O2 was condemned in September 1963 and sold to a Nottingham based scrap merchant. *(BLP - E936)*

Shortly after this picture was taken, A4 No.60013 DOMINION OF NEW ZEALAND was due to enter Doncaster works for a 'General' overhaul and the fitting of a double chimney and blastpipe. However, in this May 1958 view on Gamston curve with the Up *FLYING SCOTSMAN*, No.60013 appears 'ex-works' already. Its appearance is due to the meticulous care taken by King's Cross (Top shed) in the cleaning and preparation of its own locomotive stud. Except for eight months at Haymarket in 1937-38, and two years at Grantham from June 1948 to June 1950, this A4 spent all of its life allocated to King's Cross depot. Yes it did go into 'shops' on 20th May 1958, emerging on 4th July with a double chimney. The engine was to have two more 'General' overhauls before being withdrawn in April 1963 and then cut up at its birthplace - Doncaster works. *(BLP - E302)*

On a fine evening in May 1961 A3 No.60102 SIR FREDERICK BANBURY rests at Grantham shed after working up from King's Cross earlier in the day. Already coaled and watered, the locomotive has only to 'turn' on the triangle so that its pointing the right way home. A previous occupant of Grantham (14th June 1959 to 9th October 1960), the engine was now running out its final months from the London shed and would enter Doncaster works in November for scrapping. Originally built by the Great Northern Railway in 1922, No.60102 was rebuilt from LNER A1 type to A3 in 1942 and at the time of this photograph was the oldest of the A3's; A1/1 No.60113 GREAT NORTHERN was the oldest of the Pacific's albeit in its disfigured rebuilt state. Throughout its near forty year existence No.60102 had only two different tenders, both handsome eight-wheel GN types with two coal guards. *(BLP - E358)*

In August 1963 Neville Hill A3 No.60080 DICK TURPIN was visiting Carlisle Kingmoor and here, looking exceptionally clean, it adorns the north end of the shed yard prior to working home to Leeds. Newly arrived (June) at Neville Hill, this was not the A3's first residency in Leeds because from May 1960 it stayed at Holbeck shed for a year prior to a stint at Ardsley from where it went to Neville Hill. In December 1963 it moved to Gateshead shed and from there it was all down hill - especially the cleaning. *(BLP - E930)*

Once the preferred motive power for the Great Central line expresses, the Robinson D11's had been relegated to local and medium distance passenger workings by the 1950's. Staveley based D11 No.62663 PRINCE ALBERT was waiting to take on one such working in September 1958 when it was captured on film in the carriage sidings outside Sheffield (Victoria) station. Withdrawal was still eighteen months away for this engine but much of that period would be spent in storage. Note the lack of lining, a feature which was being gradually taken from the class starting in October 1956 with this particular engine. Condemned in May 1960, No.62663 went for cutting up at Stratford works, the only one to do so. Gorton cut up No.62665 whilst the rest of the class were dealt with at Doncaster. No.62660 BUTLER HENDERSON is of course preserved. *(BLP - E355)*

When KRP photographed Stratford based J20 No.64689 at March shed in May 1958, it had only just completed a 'General' (its last) at Stratford works but its external condition was far from immaculate. Built at Stratford in October 1922, as No.1284, it was the ultimate Great Eastern freight design and up to 1942, when they lost the crown to the Bullied Q1 'Austerity', they were the most powerful 0-6-0 type in the country with a tractive effort just over 29,000 lb. Designed by A.J.Hill, there were twenty-five engines in the class and their initial allocations took them to Cambridge and March sheds. The class first appeared in 1920 when five were produced and then in 1922 on the eve of Grouping the other twenty appeared. Although the class worked mainly from sheds bounded within the former GER territory, one engine had a ten day trial at Sheffield Neepsend shed at the end of August 1925 and in early BR days four of them went to Hornsey shed on the old GN from 1951 to 1953. However, in the early days of the LNER ten of the class were sent to Darlington works for major repairs, as opposed to the more usual venue at Stratford, and a few of those made return trips north as far as Doncaster works for other repairs. No.64689 which visited neither of the aforementioned establishments, spent all of its thirty-nine year existence on the old GER and had variously been allocated to Cambridge, Lowestoft, Ipswich, March and Stratford sheds during that time, with Stratford being its last depot before withdrawal in January 1961. *(BLP - 330)*

Seen from a somewhat unusual angle at this location, King's Cross based A4 No.60008 DWIGHT D.EISENHOWER departs Grantham with an early morning express for London in August 1962. Another preserved A4. *(BLP - E334)*

Although the Gresley O2's were the mainstay of the southern end of the ECML freight locomotive fleet, they could also be found allocated to sheds in the East Midland's area moving vast amounts of coal from the concentration yards serving the mines of Nottinghamshire and south Yorkshire. Retford based O2 No.63980 has charge of an Up freight at on Gamston curve in November 1962 and appears to be making easy work of the climb. Built as late as December 1942, into a class which had first appeared in 1918, the engine had served at numerous sheds during its twenty year life. After its initial allocation to Doncaster it moved to Colwick in January 1944 along with forty-two other members of the class, surely one of the biggest single class moves ever recorded but being wartime there must have been some strategic importance for such an event. Although many of the class had moved away from Colwick after a year, No.3850 (its original LNER number) stayed until late October 1946 when it went to Langwith Junction for a near four year stint moving even more coal. In July 1950, now with its BR number, it went to Mexborough shed from where it took coal trains over the Pennines into Lancashire where they became a common sight during this period. In February 1951 No.63980 moved back to the familiar territory of the ECML and worked from Doncaster shed for eighteen months prior to its final allocation to Retford GN shed. It was condemned in September 1963 and sold to a scrap merchant in Nottingham, its passing hardly noticed. *(BLP - E327)*

A3 No.60052 PRINCE PALATINE, buffered up to a Thompson L1 tank, awaits a Newcastle bound working at Grantham shed in August 1962. A few days after this duty the A3 entered Doncaster works for its last 'General'. As No.2551, this engine had been rebuilt from an A1 during the summer of 1941 and over the next twenty-five years, to its demise in January 1966, it managed seventeen shed moves which took it from the southern end of the ECML to GC line sheds, back to the Yorkshire section of the ECML then up to the Durham and Northumberland areas of the main line. No.60052 eventually ended its career working from St Margarets shed and was transferred there in August 1963. No doubt that move, which saw it visit Inverurie works for a three-week long 'Non-classified' repair in 1965, gave it a life extension. PRINCE PALATINE was sold for scrap in June 1966. *(BLP - E901)*

Ready to work home to London, A3 No.60107 ROYAL LANCER rests on the shed yard at Grantham in June 1961. Fitted a couple of years previously with a double blastpipe and chimney, the crews of No.60107 had constant trouble with smoke drift, even with those tiny deflectors fitted alongside the chimney. Eventually the German type trough smoke deflectors were found to eliminate the smoke problem and many of the class were fitted, albeit very late in their lives. *(BLP - E392)*

Grantham shed yard, June 1961, early evening. Resident A3 No.60047 DONOVAN, which was only two months out from a 'General' repair, is ready to take on a northbound working. Obviously, by now, Grantham depot was short of cleaners and unlike the King's Cross charges, these engines were left to accumulate filth with each outing. Fifteen months after this view was captured, No.60047 moved to New England depot where, after just six months it was condemned. Doncaster works took care of the A3 in June 1963. *(BLP - E918)*

A superb portrait of A3 No.60063 ISINGLASS at Grantham in June 1961. The King's Cross Pacific was making its way to the south end of the station to await a working that would return it to London. *(BLP - E927)*

The fifteen Peppercorn A2's, which emerged from Doncaster during the period December 1947 to August 1948, were a nice refreshing change in design from the Pacifics offered up by Thompson during his tenure as C.M.E. of the LNER. A.H.Peppercorn was a Gresley man through and through and whereas Thompson had tried his hardest to eradicate many Gresley ideas, to the detriment of many of his own designs, Peppercorn reintroduced many of the Gresley principles. The A2's were his first Pacific design and what superb looking locomotives they were. No.60533 HAPPY KNIGHT is seen here near Retford whilst working a Down express during November 1960 whilst it was allocated to Doncaster shed. Whereas the other fourteen members of the class were allocated to between two and seven sheds each during their lifetimes, No.60533 had fifteen different moves to its credit and amongst the usual venues of Copley Hill, Doncaster, Grantham and New England, there is a one week stay (2nd to 9th July 1950) at Annesley shed of all places. Now, there are not that many Eastern Pacifics which can boast that fact. Nor many named engines even amongst the B1 fraternity. Admitted, there was a few BR 'Britannia' Pacifics which called the Robin Hood hills home for a while and yes a number of ex-LMS 'Royal Scots' which, though falling apart, tended to brighten up an otherwise all-black allocation at the ex GCR shed but an Eastern Region Pacific in its prime! Wow. Perhaps it was a 'book move' and nothing became of it but who knows? If anyone can remember the event, has a photograph or can explain the presence of such a locomotive at the shed, then please contact the Publisher. No.60533 was condemned on 15th June 1963 just as the Eastern Region had declared war on steam south of Grantham. It entered Doncaster works on 2nd September 1963 for cutting up, just fifteen years old. Happily one member of the class, No.60532 BLUE PETER has been preserved. *(BLP - E331)*

Another Thompson B1 which Retford shed got from new was No.61211 and they kept hold of this one to the premature end of its fifteen year life. No.61211 was a regular engine on the Retford Up Main Line Pilot and for which job the shed staff kept the 4-6-0 in pristine condition. In June 1961 the B1 is standing in the usual position for the pilot turn, at the north end of platform 1 by the gas lamp crossing. The engine had recently returned to Retford from a 'General' overhaul at Doncaster works which no doubt contributed to its smart appearance. On Bonfire Night 1962, No.61211 went north to Doncaster for a slight repair but on being examined as it entered works, it was condemned and cut up later that month. *(BLP - E912)*

In this February 1965 scene at Haworth on the Keighley & Worth Valley Railway, preserved N2 No.69523 has just arrived from Harworth Colliery where it had been in storage since purchased from BR. There was much for the preservationists to do with this 0-6-2T before it was working once again. Compare this forty year old view with the scene at Haworth today. (BLP - E934)

In his notes for this slide, KRP described A4 No.60031 GOLDEN PLOVER as "...supershine 64B A4 with light blue nameplate..." No.60031 is approaching Grantham with the Up *ELIZABETHAN* in July 1961 and had been ex-works for four months or more so the shine was definately applied by the Haymarket shed staff. This engine had spent all of its life working from the Edinburgh depot up to this date and would continue to do so for another eight months when it went to St Rollox shed in Glasgow of all places. To work this train the A4's required a corridor tender and No.60031 had been coupled to such since building in 1937 although its first tender, No.5652, was relinquished to 4495 (60030) in February 1945 during a 'General' at Doncaster. At the completion of that repair GOLDEN PLOVER came out with tender No.5650, ex 4495, which it took to the scrapyard in December 1965. Even though it was a 65B engine from 3rd February 1962, the A4 still had a 'Non-classified', 'Casual Heavy' and a 'General' repair at Doncaster in 1962 and 1963. So, if you saw a 65B A4 working over the southern end of the ECML during this period it was only No.60031 being either borrowed or running-in. *(BLP - E931)*

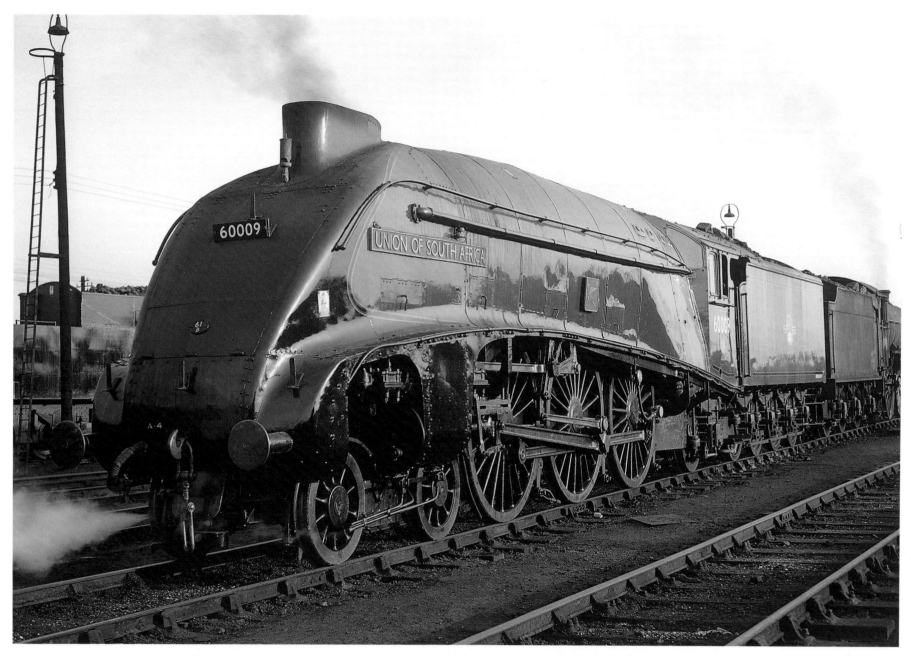

A4 No.60009 UNION OF SOUTH AFRICA was the last fully repaired ('General' overhaul) Pacific to leave Doncaster 'Plant' and is seen on Doncaster shed after that event in November 1963. By this time 60009 was allocated to Ferryhill shed in Aberdeen and on its way back to the Granite City it had to call in at Haymarket shed on the 5th December for a 'non-classified' repair, the reason for which is unknown. Haymarket was in fact its only other depot during its life. The engine had occasion to visit works again the following year and received a 'Casual Light' at Darlington which lasted from 5th February to 18th April. Another 'last' for 60009 was that it took the final A4 hauled train out of King's Cross on 24th October 1964. Of course the engine lives on in a preserved state, sometimes venturing out onto the main line ready to thrill all those who meet her. *(BLP - E354)*

Darnall based Thompson B1 No.61152 again has charge of an Up express ex Sheffield (Victoria) and is approaching Woodburn Road in August 1959. This photograph captures the steam exhaust as it expands in the early morning chill. *(BLP - E907)*

Keith Pirt had some favourite locations on the ECML from where he took many of the views featured in this album. Gamston bank near Eaton wood, just south of Retford was one of them. He liked to photograph the locomotives in full flight and this picture of Peppercorn A1 No.60142 EDWARD FLETCHER climbing the bank in August 1961 with a good exhaust whilst heading a Newcastle-King's Cross express is typical. No.60142 was one of the Heaton allocated A1's which in September 1962 moved north to Tweedmouth shed after being displaced by diesel locomotives on the bulk of the main line expresses from Newcastle. *(BLP - E365)*

Coaled, watered, cleaned out, and ready for more work, Doncaster Thompson B1 No.61087 awaits it next turn of duty at York shed in October 1964. From new in October 1946, this 4-6-0 had spent its first three years working the old Great Central main line from Darnall, Woodford and Leicester sheds. With all its repairs now completed the B1 would keep going in traffic until something happened which would render it unserviceable and therefore doomed. That event to took place on Sunday 5th December 1965. Shortly after New Years Day 1966 the engine was sold to the Chesterfield scrap yard of Garnham, Harris & Elton. *(BLP - E937)*

Barring the obvious exceptions, many A4's have featured in this album and here we present 'Top shed's' No.60021 WILD SWAN south of Stoke tunnel in August 1962 with a King's Cross bound express. The engine was on its way home from Doncaster after a 'Casual Light' and its penultimate repair. No.60021 was at 'the Cross' when that shed was due for closure and so, like many of the residents, it moved to New England where its services were not really required. Within weeks it was laid up and then, in October, condemned. The end came at Doncaster works during the following January. *(BLP - E920)*